I'M A KID BUT I'M NOT KIDDIN'
[Tru dat]

I LOVE THE LORD

By
Crystaline Joi Prothro
13 years old

We have nerves too!!!

Youth is not a yoke.

Have you ever been young?

Mom, dad, don't worry, when I grow up I'll put away childish things.

Robot Publishing
A Division of JADOPRECRYS Enterprise
P.O. Box 961840 – Riverdale, GA 30296

I'm A Kid But I'm Not Kiddin'

Copyright © August 1998 by Robot Publishing

All scripture quotations in this book, except those noted otherwise, are from the Open Bible, King James Version, Thomas Nelson, Publisher.

Published by Robot Publishing Company
PO Box 961840 Riverdale, GA 30296
A division of JADOPRECRYS Enterprise

All rights reserved. No part of this publication may be reproduced, stored in a retrieval system or transmitted in any form by any means, electronic, mechanical, photocopy, recording or otherwise, without the prior permission of the publisher, except as provided by USA Copyright law.

Cover design – Robot Publishing Company
First Printing – August 1998
Printed in the United States of America
ISBN 0-9662919-3-X

All rights reserved.
Printed in the United States of America

3212 East Highway 30 • Kearney, NE 68847 • 1-800-650-7888

ACKNOWLEDGEMENT

I would like to acknowledge all who have been very kind in helping me to say what I hope is very meaningful to my readers. I would like to thank my dad and mom, Apostle and Mrs. James S. Prothro, my big sister, Precious, my little brother Sir James Spe´cial´ and two special sisters to me, Pastor Rosalynn A. Curry and Prophetess LaJunne Smith. Thanks also to my friends TeErica Walker and MiShae Smith for sharing their stories with me and allowing me to share them with you. God bless you all.

A very special appreciation to my grown up kid sister, my ice cream partner, my international connection, free lunch at Red Lobster sister, Charmaine Johnson.

I would like to dedicate this book to my mom and dad who were the source of my motivation to write this book and share my life. Thanks for letting me speak out so freely. I love you.

Table Of Contents

Acknowledgment	*Page 3*
Forward	*Page 5*
Preface	*Page 9*
Introduction	*Page 13*
Parents Examination Of Selfishness	*Page 17*
I'm Not Kiddin'	*Page 19*
Salvation Can Be A Struggle	*Page 27*
More Of The Same	*Page 37*
Other Kids' Points Of View	*Page 49*
Adjusting The "Tude"	*Page 63*
A Kid-O-Gram	*Page 76*
Reality In A Dream	*Page 77*
Setting Goals Is The First Step To Progress	*Page 95*

FORWARD

By Apostle James S. Prothro

I wish that I could do something about the irresponsible decision to take prayer out of our schools. I wish, secondly, that I could change what has happened to our young people as it relates to the church. Their chances of survival have been minimized by adult decisions of self-centeredness, spiritual apathy, financial complacency, and common salvation.

For instance, it is almost a given that a parent, who will not go to church, will not enforce his child's church attendance for fear of the image of hypocrisy. This is an extremely neglectful and mentally dangerous thing to do to a child. With peer pressure being as it is and so much worldliness being introduced to them, parents need to take every opportunity that they have to encourage their children to get closer to God.

We should really look at our scale of involvement as it relates to our children and see just how much worldliness we entertain with them as opposed to how much church time we share with them. We ought to think about what really happens when we go to club-type settings with our children, when we allow them to smoke as long as they do it in the house, and drink as long as they keep it moderate.

We also allow them to have company in privacy, in darkness, and in seclusion, as long as they do not make noise and wake us up because we have to go to work the next morning.

Our children are our future. Our concern and our sensitivity toward their vulnerability leave a lot to be desired. Regardless of what the skeptics, sociologists, and agnostics believe, church is still the best teaching institution there is. It is better than any Rehabilitation Center, Alcoholics Anonymous or Narcotics/Cocaine Anonymous. Church was intended to be the place where a child learns in the nurture and admonition of God (Ephesians 6:4). It has been turned into a common place of theatrics, into a Singles Ministry where you can find someone to date and eventually marry, or, unfortunately, many more things including a place to cry about how bad life is.

This is not how God intended for our children to be raised as it relates to spirituality. Our kids need to know about Jesus: why He died, how He died, when He died, and where He died. They need to know about the death, burial, and resurrection because that, and only that, is the gospel.

I wish to challenge parents everywhere to firstly, introduce this book to your children with an apology for neglect of duty, if applicable. Secondly, make a commitment to help them in their struggle and their endeavor to get through this life of distractions and disappointments. Thirdly, we must reinforce the Bible and the church, which are the true virtues of life. It is good to reward the smaller kids when they learn memory verses and compliment them when we hear them singing spiritual songs, hoping that spiritual songs will become their choice of entertainment.

I challenge you to allow gospel singing and spiritual music to rule your home again. If we do not control the television programs that induce contemporary rap music, involving lewd dancing and profanity, then we may lose our children to Satan. Teach them hymns. Yes, those old boring hymns can still be beneficial to a young contemporary society. These spiritual oldie goldies can help our children, even in unconscious development. This alone makes their lives worthwhile. It is better than just letting them sit around and listen to music that is sometimes satanic. Our children, as it relates to music, are desperately in need of guidance and direction.

Please help your children to shape their Christian lives in the way that Jesus would have them to be. Help them to know that the struggles of life can be handled and Jesus is always there for them. Reinforce chastisement, but let us ask God constantly for wisdom so that we will not create psychological reasons for them not to like us.

May God help us in our endeavor to raise our children. Certainly we have a long way to go. I guess, to each and every individual family, the question has become to punish or not to punish? I cannot advocate breaking the law, as it relates to chastisement neither do I suggest that anyone should. I still think that no one knows you and your child's relationship like God does. Go to God in prayer and do what is best for your child, knowing that he will thank you for his corrections down the road. The Bible reads in Proverbs 22:15, "Foolishness is bound in the heart of a child; but the rod of correction shall drive it far from him." Also in Proverbs 13:24 it says, "He that spareth his rod hateth his son...." I do not believe that the rod and verbal reproof are the only ways to discipline. Certainly there are other means but we must make sure that these means are effective.

Now the new and modern way of thinking is that chastisement, as we know it, is not good for the child sociologically. Again, I am not a sociologist and do not intend to suggest sociology to anyone. I do know that you know your child and you are the one that lie in bed and listen to his cries in the midnight hour from mistakes that he has made.

Pray and acknowledge God and He will direct your path.

PREFACE

By Precious M. Prothro

Growing up is not "peaches and cream" as people relay it to be. There are physical, emotional and psychological transitions. These may be unfamiliar to our conscience awareness, although we are constantly hearing about them. We go from newborn to toddler, toddler to child, child to adolescent, adolescent to adult.

During the first years of youthfulness there are many outside transitions that can cause a positive and/or negative effect: moving from grade to grade, teacher to teacher, friend to friend, school to school, and maybe even neighborhood to neighborhood. All of these changes bring along with them their own new set of trials, rules, and heartaches.

A two-year old may see the endeavor of going to the potty as a not so invigorating yet challenging experience. A thirteen year old may see the changes in their sexual nature as an invigorating and interesting achievement. Growth can be somewhat confusing.

While a thirteen year old may find a two-year old's success as minute, a two-year old could not even begin to comprehend a thirteen year old's problem.

Change can often be confusing, lonely, very dark, and misunderstood by our youth.

It seems as though a child who has no bills, no husband/wife, no children, no car, etc. should never have a worry in the world. To the contrary, that is not at all the accurate assumption of youthfulness.

I have found that most of the pressure that comes with growing up is in striving to please others: parents, teachers, mentors, friends (of the same and opposite sex), etc.... However, in the midst of all those people, very infrequently, if at all, comes the thought, "Am I pleasing God?" I was saved at the age of seven and though I had developed an intimate consciousness about God, He was not who I was concerned about at first.

I heard the scriptures of Romans 8:28, Colossians 2:10, I John 4:4, and of course Philippians 4:13, yet it was not enough for me. My problems were bigger than the mentioning of mere words. (These are the thoughts of youthfulness.) Parents, pastors, teachers, and mentors are all important but we think the most important people to please, during youthfulness, are our friends.

Mom and Dad will love me regardless. Siblings have to love me. Pastors, teachers, and mentors are required to be there for me no matter what. However, my friends may leave me if I do not do this or that the way they would like for me to do it. There is also another perspective, the one in which I was a part of, but no longer. In the past, if friends would not do what I wanted them to do or act the way that I wanted them to act then they would no longer be my friends.

Most youth think to do right (if taught to do right), know to do right, and even fear the consequences of not doing right. Yet, the desire to please friends and peers is much greater. Friends can and are most often detrimental to and for our lives. They, though not intentional, are often hindrances rather than help. Through experience I have learned what my parents tried to tell me for years, "Your best friend can be your worst enemy." However, it has taken twenty-one years for me to recognize this truth. Why I did not realize it when they first said it, thus eliminating so many heart-crushing experiences, is an easy answer for an adult but a stumbling challenge for a child.

Youthfulness often causes unwise decisions and mistakes. It is because, as Apostle Prothro says in the book he authored entitled, **Man, God's Robot**, "Youth is a continual intoxication; it is the fever of reason; the cold of common sense; the flu of fruition; the virus of virtue; the pimple of power; the rash of rationale; and the pneumonia of new life." Apostle Prothro often asks the question, "Why can't we have one youth who takes the words of an older person, 'if

I had known then what I know now.'" If they would make up their minds and commit to escaping that truth they could devote time to learning from others' experiences.

Why not take the advice and experience of someone who has "been there done that?" Youthfulness, from an adult's viewpoint, should be remembered not renounced, treasured not taunted, and salvaged not severed. It is not an event to be forgotten but one to be remembered, thus lending a helping hand to as many youth as possible. For adults, our past experiences, hurts, fears, and all other situations must be taken to God, thus we receive help and deliverance so that we can help someone else. No matter how long it has been, how old we are, or how hard the situation was, our experiences should be taken and used toward rescuing another youth from the same.

This young author is my baby sister. How much I love her is incapable of being known. I am proud that she has obeyed life's requirement for her purpose.

Thank you Chrissy for being honest and sincere. May you write many more books. The world really needs your talent.

Your sister,

Precious M. Prothro

Precious M. Prothro

P.S. Please return my jewelry, clothes, money, makeup, etc.

INTRODUCTION

From the Heart of a Parent

We are headed for the 21st century and things are going really fast. It is impossible to differentiate the present from the past unless we look into the future. The future is in the hands of the generation that this author represents. We have gross governmental problems thus we cannot afford to overlook the outlook of the younger generation.

Truth is spoken in this book. Reality is dealt with. Life is laid out as it relates to children, young adults, and adolescents. It is time to listen to our youth. Reading this book will award you the knowledge that you will need to help you understand how your children think. They are not packages. They are real humans with feelings and opinions. Their view of church and God is expressed in this book.

My congratulations and compliments to this great young author who, no doubt, had a difficult time expressing what she feels. How did we come to think that we know what our children really feel based on our past childhood? Things are different.

Thank God He doesn't change. Satan controls this world we live in. The world is our society and its organized selfish principles, improper motives, and unworthy standard of value; it is a system of thought and conduct that does not give God His rightful place. For a young person it can be an attractive allurement that turns into a wilderness of trouble.

When young people talk, we should really listen. Please let me add, without bias, that they are afraid to talk to us for fear of our reaction. Not to mention, we lie to them about not being mad at what we hear. I wonder if we could handle the truth when we receive it? Probably not. Let's stop searching for the proper game to use that will aid us in tricking our children into telling us things that we cannot handle. Ask, and if you receive, be understanding and merciful (do not forget your past and the many mistakes you made). Seek, and when you find, control yourself. Knock, and do not come in unless they tell you to. They deserve their privacy.

Rules that children establish are very fair. Do unto them as you ask them to do to you; do not eavesdrop during their phone calls; do not read their diaries; do not search through their room without their knowledge; do not embarrass them unnecessarily in front of their friends; do not let them ride without seat belts; do not drink with them; do not buy them cigarettes; do not allow them to become lazy; do not spoil them with things that are detrimental to their future; do not forget to love them; and most of all do not forget to live the life of a true Christian before them. Please enjoy this book. I did. This author may be a kid, but she's not kidding, she really loves the Lord.

*Isaiah 40:30 Even the **youths** shall faint and be weary, and the **young** men shall utterly fall.*

*Ecclesiastes 12:1 Remember now thy Creator in the days of thy **youth**, while the evil days come not, nor the years draw nigh, when thou shalt say, I have no pleasure in them.*

PARENTS THINK THIS BOOK IS BEAUTIFULLY PREPARED AND MORALLY SOUND.

KIDS JUST THINK IT'S COOL!!!

PARENTS' EXAMINATION OF SELFISHNESS

1. When you get on my case about being an "A" student is it because you will have the pleasure of riding around in the neighborhood with a bumper sticker that reads "MY CHILD MADE THE HONOR ROLL?"

2. Why do you hug and kiss me more in public than you do at home? Are you trying to impress someone?

3. What is the true motivation for you wanting me to brush my teeth: healthy and strong gums or the responsibility of a dental bill?

4. Why are all of my chest pains perceived as chest pains? Maybe it's my heart trembling for your love.

5. Why can't I have company? Is it really not a cool thing to do or do I remind you of yourself?

6. What is the real reason you will not teach me about sex?

7. Why is my room different from yours as it relates to being clean?

8. Why is it wrong for me to curse, drink, or smoke but it is okay for you to do?

9. Have you shared everything with me about my birth that I need to know?

10. If I told you the truth, could you handle it?

P.S. I have found the best way to give advice to your children is to find out what they want and then advise them how to do it. **Harry S. Truman**

*Psalm 103:5 Who satisfieth thy mouth with good things; so that thy **youth** is renewed like the eagle's.*

I'M NOT KIDDIN'

Hello, my name is Chrissy Prothro and I want to tell you some real "411," better known as information. **Loving God is some serious stuff.** You really have to have your act together if you intend to make it to the end without getting distracted and turned around. Wherever the end is, I don't know.

> **I can't understand why all men do not love this idea of coming to God.**

To me the place you make it to isn't as important as the person you make it with. (You know what I'm saying?) Of course the person I'm talking about is Jesus. I wish I could say Jesus was a household word but I can't because every household doesn't accept Him. I wish everyone could love Him like I do. Please do not try to tell me that I don't know what I'm talking about simply because I'm so young. Jesus was a master at suffering little children to come unto Him. My daddy teaches that suffering means to allow, permit, or tolerate, so regardless of what my age is I'm still invited by God to come to Him. **I can't understand why all men do not love this idea of coming to God.**

Loving God is some serious stuff.

> **It's not easy being a preacher's child, especially when your parents are sold out to God.**

Please excuse me. Earlier I used the word "can't." My dad doesn't like that word. He teaches me that I can do all things through Christ which strengthens me (Philippians 4: 13). You can also and it doesn't matter if you're a kid or an adult. I'm sorry if I offend anyone but I just want to share with you my life from a preacher's child's point of view, and from the point of view of a youth serving God. Believe me, **it's not easy being a preacher's child, especially when your parents are sold out to God.** This is not meant to sound like a negative position rather a realistic opinion of mine. It's really hard, but we'll be okay, for real.

I believe I have it harder than most teenagers do in that I am a preacher's child. I am always worrying that if I do something wrong then someone will tell me, "Oh that's not how a preacher's child should act."

You're talking about pressure! That's the real deal! They should see how they act. I think everyone needs to

> **Parents aren't always right about us but they do love us.**

> **We are asked to trust our parents but can we really trust them? Can they really trust us?**

be real all the time, although we aren't. We need to pray anyway, like I'm learning to do. Parents think that because they think they know us, they do. May I share this piece of advice with you? As long as you think you know us you may eliminate the possibility of learning about us.

Parents aren't always right about us but they do love us. It seems to be hard for them to admit to being wrong and "Oh" how we need them to apologize when they are. Unfortunately many times they don't. I understand why so many of my friends are afraid to talk to their parents; it's not an easy thing to do. We all need to remember that it's not easy for one generation to understand the next. For instance trust. As children, **we are asked to trust our parents but can we really trust them? Can they really trust us?** I do not agree that we should be friends above being parent and child. However, we should be allowed to talk without the fear of being hit, abused, and, in some cases, cursed out.

The majority of our friends will tell us not to trust our parents and the majority of their friends will tell them not to trust us. Who wins? **How do we fix this problem?**

Here is my opinion. First, each family varies. No two families are alike. What works for one may not work for the other but we can make a rule for all of us to start with.

> **Parents do not deserve disrespect just because we're pouting.**

What if we made rules that say:

1) Listen to one another
2) Respect one another's opinions
3) Do not play games with one another
4) Do not take advantage of your position.

I was saved at the age of eleven and I've been in church all my life. I haven't always liked being in church but I try never to show it. You may say why not show it if you feel it? Well, my parents work hard to show me the right way. **Parents do not deserve disrespect just because we're pouting.**

Some teenagers think that they should have a choice as to whether or not they should go to church. Parents think differently. I kind of understand them be-

> **How do we fix this problem?**

> **Too many teens try to live a "godly" life as well as a "worldly" life.**

cause I probably would not have always gone on my own. We must be fair. They know what's best for us.

Consider this question. If our parents let us choose, who is to say that we'll choose to go to church? Some people say that if we go to church against our own will when we are young, then when we get older we will rebel against the church and not love God anymore. I don't think so. I think that once you are really saved, it doesn't matter who makes you go to church because you'll be excited about what you get out of the sermon.

Too many teens try to live a "godly" life as well as a "worldly" life. We may be young but we must decide on who we are going to serve. I'm sure there are plenty of us that go through the same thing mentally. We love the Lord and go to church two or three times a week; but on the other hand we lie, cheat, and fight throughout the week. This lifestyle can get very confusing. It is always true that Satan tempts us to put off church instead of putting off the wrong things that we do. Believe me, I know what you're going through. I've been there, but if you wait it out you'll see that God is the better way to go.

I go through the same things most teenagers go through: color prejudices, peer pressure, trying to have a social life, and concentrating on school and God at the same time. **I know it's hard but if we stay with God He will direct our paths (Proverbs 3:5-6).**

> **Many people have been made to think that church is only for nerds who are not happy.**

There are plenty of people who have done everything from having sex to doing drugs to running away from home. Although I haven't gone through any of those things, for anyone who has, I want you to know that it's going to be okay as long as you stay with God.

That is the hard part, staying with God and keeping Him on your mind while being tempted with so much stuff. To make it worse you may be jumped on or beaten up if you are nerdish. Most definitely you will be laughed at. **Many people have been made to think that church is only for nerds who are not happy.**

> **I know it's hard but if we stay with God He will direct our paths (Proverbs 3:5-6).**

All teenagers cannot handle

> **We need our parents and they need us.**

the pressure of being laughed at and picked on. Many fight back by keeping to themselves or refusing to play with others for fear of being picked on. I'm sure it happened in our parents' time and I'm sure that they dealt with it in the same way. **Two wrongs don't make a right.**

As teenagers, we must learn to trust God. He will help us get through these tough times of adolescence. I pray for everybody that God will help us to understand other people. **We need our parents and they need us.**

Everyone reading this book will not agree with my writings. Please try to understand from my age bracket. I'm a kid but I'm not kidding, I truly love the Lord. He makes me feel happy and excited especially when He wakes me up in the morning through the alarm clock. I realize that it's not the clock but His love towards me, His grace upon me, and His will for me. These are some of the good things I get from being saved.

> **Two wrongs don't make a right.**

Don't forget to remember that Adam and Eve disobeyed God, which caused

God to send His son Jesus to die on the cross for our sins to put us back like they were in the Garden of Eden.

*I Kings 18:12 ...but I thy servant fear the Lord from my **youth**.*

*Judges 8:20b ...for he feared, because he was yet a **youth**.*

Salvation can be a struggle for young people
(Can you feel me?)

The first thing I want to share with my readers is my view of salvation. I want to share with you five points of view:

- Confession – Acts 2:21
- Repentance – St. Mark 1:15
- Faith – St. John 3:14-36
- Regeneration – St. John 3:3-8
- Scripture – 2 Timothy 3:15

I looked in Webster's Dictionary, so I could get help because I didn't want to write anything that wasn't true. The definition for the word *confess,* in the dictionary, is to "fess" up to your sins to God in order to get a ticket to get into heaven. (I changed the words into kids' language.) I believe that you've got to have a ticket in order to get in. Jesus stands at the door to take your ticket. That's the reason Jesus died on the cross. He has the job of ticket-taker. He has to take your ticket for you, because you can't hand it straight to God. It's sort of like when you go to a movie. The guy takes your ticket after you buy it. We were born into a world of sin. Jesus will take away our sins if we hand them to Him through repenting and receiving Him as our Lord.

A lot of people don't know that they are guilty of the Adam sin in the Garden of Eden. I didn't either before I started writing this book. My daddy sat me down in front of him, in his office, which is the most frightening place you can be unless you really mean business about learning, and he drilled me and drilled me. Tears came to my eyes but he kept drilling me on salvation. He wanted me to get a clear picture of what salvation really is and really means. I knew some basic things but now I understand that because of what Adam and Eve did, all of mankind has to confess that they too are guilty of sin. If they confess and recognize the fact that Jesus died on the cross and paid the price for sin then all they have to do is to receive Him into their hearts and be saved. Then they can feel the assurance that I have today, and my confession can now trade places with profession.

Before now I could only say that I'm a sinner. I have in me the seed of Adam and Eve. But now that I have gone by way of Jesus, I now profess that I'm saved and I'm no longer guilty of the sin of Adam and Eve. So my confession leads to my profession. I now profess that I'm saved and I am glad.

I don't mean to sound like I'm rapping or anything. I just want to make it very clear that confession and profession are necessary for those who are saved. Once again, Adam and Eve messed it up for us. They really got us in trouble. God didn't want us to stay in trouble so He sent Jesus through Mary, and He was born. Your parents can explain this a little better. Jesus said, I know that you guys are in trouble, but I've come to get you out of trouble if you want me to. Then He said, Anybody who wants to just receive me as his friend in his heart and soul, I'll die for him so he won't have to die and go to the devil's home. I try not to make it a practice saying the name of the devil's home. Jesus died for mankind. The debt has been paid for those who receive Him as their friend. So the sins that Adam and Eve got themselves in trouble with will no longer be upon their heads. Praise God that's really, really good! I think that's why they call the Bible the "good news" because it's good stuff.

That's all I really want to say about confess, and now I want to talk about believing in your *heart* that God raised Jesus from the dead. (Romans 10: 9) This was kind of hard for me to understand at first because when you start talking about people being raised from the dead that gets a little weird you know and starts to sound like a joke. What it means is God asked us to do two things: confess Adam's sin and then really believe in our hearts that Jesus died for us.

Now what if we believed that Jesus died for us but He stayed on the cross? That really wouldn't do us much good. God wants us not only to believe that He died for us but that He was buried. God promised that He would raise Him from the dead. When we believe that God actually did this, we can believe that when

He was raised from the dead, He was raised so that those of us who take Him as our friend, into our hearts and souls, will have a place to go and live with Him throughout eternity.

So to believe in your heart that God raised Him from the dead is necessary. You've got to believe this. You can't play around with it. This is not something that you say or something that you can joke about, but you've really got to believe in your heart that Jesus died and that God raised Him from the dead. Then the Bible says you would have put an end to your worrying about salvation. That doesn't mean that you'll die. It means that you don't have to worry about being saved anymore because you would have already done everything that it takes to be saved.

Another thing that I want to add about the heart is that if Jesus is in your heart then He can help you so that you won't let anything get into your heart and mess with your mind and tear up your life. You won't let boyfriends and girlfriends get into your heart and just mess up the way you feel about other people. A lot of people have gotten out of control with this boyfriend and girlfriend thing. When their hearts get involved, it's hard for anything else to get in their hearts. God wants your heart. He wants to make sure that you're going to be okay.

Confession is when someone has done wrong and they need to tell someone about it in hopes of getting it right. According to the Bible, we have to confess to God by way of Jesus' name, "...no man cometh unto the Father but by me." (St. John 14:6) Sometimes it's hard to confess because you are embarrassed about what you did. As teenagers, who can we trust with our confessions? Not everyone can keep a secret. I may get in trouble for what I'm about to say here but it's the truth anyway. When our parents correct us are they getting on our cases for what we have done or are they just reminded of what they did in their past? It does not matter what age we are no one should be a hypocrite. According to the Bible, St. John 8:32 says, "And ye shall know the truth, and the truth shall make you free."

The language between a parent and a child is so wide that both parties should be willing to listen to and try to understand the other. However, that's not always the case. Since it is so much easier to hide from life as a child, too often that's what we do. For instance, someone in your class at school could touch you in an inappropriate place. It can cause you to cry really hard. When your parents ask if there is something wrong with you, it will seem easier to hide by saying something that is not true. I can almost bet you (my dad would kill me if I did though, so put your money back in your pocket) all you'll have to do when you get in your parents' presence is lie and say that you have a tummy ache. They will offer you Pepto-Bismol. Unless they search they will never find your pain.

Would someone please answer this question? Shouldn't our parents know when something like that is going on with us? This may be asking too much. Moms, dads, please forgive us if we are putting too much pressure on you. We just want to know that you can tell when something has happened that we don't want to tell anyone about.

What I'm trying to say is that our ability to detect our parents' problems and theirs to detect ours is off course. Sometimes I think that although they love us they have absolutely no idea of how hard it is being a teenager in these times. It's not their fault because if we were asked to live in their generation with our present knowledge we would be bored to death as they are scared to death.

Let's try to understand them from their standpoint. It's gonna be hard but we must try. Our parents have a major responsibility. They have to feed us when we're hungry, buy us more clothes when we grow out of the ones we're wearing, buy us expensive shoes because we wanna look good and keep up with the latest styles, and pay rent so we'll have somewhere to stay.

Last but not least, please parents, keep a phone in the house, excuse me…in my room.
<u>Consider this for laughter:</u>

We will not talk on the phone after 10:00pm and not before then, unless we have finished our homework. We will be in the bed at 9:30pm every night and we will not watch TV after 10:00pm. We won't try to date until we're 25. We won't waste money and we will not have idol rap singers nor infatuations with athletes and grown folks.

Now let's get down to business again. To our parents we wish to write this letter:

Dear Parents,
I know you've got it hard trying to take care of my business and manage life at the same time. The Bible says in Proverbs 3:6, "In all thy ways acknowledge him, and he shall direct thy paths." Also in Romans 8:28, "And we know that all things work together for good to them that love God, to them who are the called according to his purpose." If you have a moment I would like to confess something to you. I confess that I am your child; at least that's what you've told me. I have taken your word and am honored to be your child. I confess that I am expensive but I am your responsibility. I have serious attitudes; I wonder where I get them from? You seem to be proud of me when people say I look like you, but then you get upset with me when I act like you. I confess that many of the things I do are the very same things that you did when you were my age. I confess that I talk behind your back. Sometimes I wonder if you ever did that yourself. I confess that I don't tell

you everything because in my opinion you couldn't handle it. This is not a "bust" so don't feel like you have to fuss. I confess most of all that I love you very, very much and that I'm so glad that you are mine and I am yours.

>Sincerely yours,
>Your biological transfer

Now I want to share five scriptures on **confession**. Please read them and get them into your hearts.

1. *St. Matthew 10:32,* "Whosoever therefore shall confess me before men, him will I confess also before my Father which is in heaven."
2. *Romans 10:9,* "That if thou shalt confess with thy mouth the Lord Jesus, and shalt believe in thine heart that God hath raised him from the dead, thou shalt be saved."
3. *Romans 14:11,* "For it is written, As I live, saith the Lord, every knee shall bow to me, and every tongue shall confess to God."
4. *James 5:16,* "Confess your faults one to another, and pray one for another, that ye may be healed. The effectual fervent prayer of a righteous man availeth much."
5. *I John 1:9,* "If we confess our sins, he is faithful and just to forgive us our sins, and to cleanse us from all unrighteousness."

The Bible says in Acts 2:21, "And it shall come to pass, that whosoever shall call on the name of the Lord shall be *saved*."

Salvation is something that could really help us in our relationship with our parents if we are to save our relationship throughout this tough time of puberty and adolescence. We all must confess that we need the Lord Jesus to get into the midst of our relationship, hold our hands as a unit, and guide us through these tough times.

Now let us talk about St. Matthew 10:32, which is saying that whoever confesses their love for Jesus, He in return will confess them before His Father in heaven. We should not be embarrassed to say that we know Jesus and that we go to church although sometimes there is much pressure in saying we can't do something that other kids are doing, only because we're saved.

Being saved is not enough. We still have to read our Bibles and pray every day. There are probably some people that think that because they are saved they don't have to do these things. Well, that's not true. These are daily chores and obligations. If we do these things then we will keep ourselves out of trouble with God and out of the devil's hands.

I'm sure that all saved people have had at least one time (I hope many more) where they have felt the

Holy Ghost. (Some call it the Holy Spirit. We all believe that spirits are ghosts anyway.) If you have, you know how important it is to maintain a relationship with Jesus as your Savior. We cannot let dating, styles, music, drugs, etc. draw us away from God.

Now let us look at the second scripture. In Romans 10:9 it says, "That if thou shalt confess with thy mouth the Lord Jesus, and shalt believe in thine heart that God hath raised him from the dead, thou shalt be saved."

In this scripture we have two important things that we must do. One is that we should confess the Lord Jesus and two is to believe in our hearts that God raised Him from the dead. Then the Bible promises us that if we do this we will be saved. There are so many things to distract us from being saved, so much worldly entertainment. Let's keep focused.

MORE OF THE SAME

Another issue I want to face is television. I want to talk about how television can get down into our systems and mess up our minds. None of the shows or commercials have anything to do with God. There might be three or four that do, but most of them do not. Commercials these days have to do with cigarettes and psychic hotlines. We all know that nobody knows everything except God. Most of these television shows are really nothing but a commercial about cigarettes telling you that they can relax you but that's not true. Cigarettes actually get down into your lungs and can cause you to die. They don't put that in the commercials because they want you to buy their product.

They've also put smoking on cartoons and they know that everyone watches cartoons or almost all kids. That makes kids think that it's okay to smoke but it's not. Also, parents smoke around their kids which makes the kids think that it's safe to smoke. Once again, it's not.

There are also shows, movies, and even cartoons that have cursing in them. That's letting kids know that it's okay to curse, but it's not.

I believe that we can win over these temptations that come through not only television but also the environment that we are sometimes in. I don't want to use the phrase "hang around" because we don't always choose to be at some of the places that our parents take us.

There are so many things happening in school but we have to go to school. The devil is always tempting people who are trying to teach you how to curse, how to smoke, how to do drugs, and yes, how to have sex. I'm concerned about so many of my friends who are showing an interest in having sex. I pray that all of us will please wait until we're married and make sure that the first time that we kiss boys or they kiss us (girls) is when the preacher says, "Now you may kiss the bride."

I believe that we can win but we've got to make good decisions. The Bible says in James 1:14 that the devil tempts us with evil. God doesn't do that because He does not like evil. The devil tempts us and draws us away from God because he knows our desires. He watches us when we're watching television and the way we respond. He watches us when we're dancing and the way we dance, and so he gets the "411" on us. Instead of us taking him as a "911" we are quick to think that he does not exist.

He does exist and we must make up our minds about which way we're going. Are we going the right way or the wrong way? My dad always says, "indecision never wins." We've got to make decisions to do right and be firm with that. We have to be determined not to let anyone lead us to do wrong, tell us to do wrong, or put drugs, cigarettes or alcohol in our hands.

As young Christians we've got to keep our bodies as the temples (house, place were God lives) of God. And we can do it. I know we can! It is necessary that we do. Also, we've got to start having devotion. Some may call it quiet time. When we get up in the morning, it's vital that we first pray before we brush our teeth or any of that other kind of stuff. Pray and thank God for letting us wake up and then we can have devotion. We can read a scripture and sing a song and just have quiet time. I know it'll help you through the day.

It's tough doing this everyday because sometimes when you wake up you're extremely tired because you stayed up so late the night before. So that's another area in our lives that we've got to learn to control.

Isn't it interesting how the devil makes us think that our parents are being bad parents when they make us go to bed to get proper rest? Then in the mornings when we should be getting up with joy, we get up with guess what? You guessed it right, "attitudes." I believe that if we would get close to God then He'll take care of us. He won't let the devil destroy us. He hears our prayers regardless of how young we are. God hears our prayers.

So we've just got to ask Him to help us to overcome more and more of the temptations that we have to deal with in school. Then we have to believe that God is not going to tell us a lie. He's going to do exactly what He says He's going to do. He's going to take care of His children. His promises never fail. Even Jesus, when He was tempted, stood on the promises of God. I believe that all of us regardless of how young we are can get better at the things that we're doing if we stand on the promises of God.

Often we hear the word discipline. We hear it when we're at school in P.E. (Physical Education). We hear our teachers saying that we need to be more disciplined. I think it means we have to be more in control of our lives. We need to make decisions based on the good knowledge that we have and not the bad. The Bible says that we are blessed if we make it through the things we're tempted with, without yielding to the enemy. (James 1:12)

We've got to stay away from all of the sinful things that give us pleasure. When someone tells us how good it is and how nice it is to be high from drugs and alcohol, we've got to learn how to first say "no" and then to stay away from those people who are bad influences. That's the devil's territory and we shouldn't live there. We must set rules for ourselves. There are certain things we should not do and certain places we should not go. I have set several rules for myself. There are certain things I am not going to do until I get married. There are certain things I'm not going to allow anyone to make me do, having sex being one of those things. I won't talk about dating until my parents say I can date.

There are just certain rules I have set for myself and I practice these rules. Sometimes I feel the pressure from my friends because maybe all of them have not set these same rules. But I thank God that I'm saved and in that I'm saved I have a special power and a special strength to help me make it through these tough times as a youngster. It's not easy for any of us but the devil is "really" after those of us that he does not have yet. With discipline and self-control we're going to win this battle. We've got to learn how to say "no" to the devil.

One day my daddy was preaching. I remember it so clearly. He said that, "you have to say 'no' long enough so that the devil can feel your resistance." Then he will run from you instead of you running from him.

I was a little confused at first but now that I think about it, it's like when somebody wants to play with your toys or your books or your balls and you tell them, "I don't think so." To them, that may mean they can. Then they may get your stuff and you get upset with them. Although it's not good to do this, you may jerk it from them. Then they'll know that you are serious.

Sometimes the devil will take what God has given to you, your mom and dad, your teachers, and other adults that are good for you, and make you think that they are not good for you. You have to go back and tell the devil that he's not going to do that to you. You're going to accept what's good for you as good and that you're going to resist him.

In James 4:7, the Bible says that if I resist the devil the devil will tuck his tail and run from me. I like that! I may be a kid but I'm not kidding. I really like that! I believe that the one thing the devil wants to steal from us is our minds and the desire to do hard work. We've got to work hard if we want to make it because the devil wants us to grow up and have nothing in life and be a "nobody." He wants us to live on the streets and be drug addicts and alcoholics.

If we work hard then God rewards us. I know that sometimes we want to go out and play like all the rest of the kids, but first we need to check and see if we have done our chores and our homework. Most of all have we prayed and gotten our lives in order with God?

I want to say that it is very important to pay careful attention to the things that are going on around us. When we are at the dinner table eating with our family we should really listen to the things that they say and the things that they try to tell us. Some of these things may make you mad but you should still listen because they're good for you. If you don't listen you might get in trouble. I think the message goes like this, "If you make your bed hard you'll have to lay in it." I would rather think it should go like this, "If you don't make up your bed, you'd better pray because Mommy is on her way." (You know what I mean.)

I believe that God has given us, even while we are young, power and authority. I also believe that if we would stop singing so many blues songs and saying words we have no business saying, and start quoting the scriptures and calling on the name of Jesus, then the devil would recognize us as being strong kids. He'll know that although we are kids, we are not kidding, we really love the Lord!

I keep hearing talk about no more Social Security and no more retirement plans. I'm not sure what all of that means but I do know that if I stay with God He's gonna take care of me. If you were to look in my closet you would see how God has taken care of me. I may not have what everybody else has but I've got more than what I really need. I've also picked up a little weight so that tells you that I'm eating well, and I don't exercise like I should! Young people, we've got to exercise to keep our bodies strong so that if the devil comes and try to make us sick or give us a disease, our bodies can fight against it.

We've got to watch what we eat. Although we love junk food, it's not good for us. Braces are on the way, and cavities, when we eat a lot of sugar and junk food; boy those things hurt. If we are to survive and get by then we'll have to do better than we're doing with our eating habits. Our habits are not very good.

I remembered when I was younger, deciding that certain things were not good for me. Most of them were things I heard other people say weren't good for them. I have not figured out this thing about spinach yet. Parents and the adults say that it's good for us but we know it's not good to us.

How do we get past what we know and start trusting what other people say? I think that we can do this if we recognize that what we know is not but part of what we can know. Our parents are smarter than we are and we can't slick them because they've already created the laws of oatmeal and grease. (I hope you get my "slick" point.) They know the tricks. They know the avenues we travel. They know the games we play. There's no need in disrespecting our parents by lying to them and trying to play games. If you do wrong try to talk with somebody and get help so you won't do it again.

I think Jesus loves it when He helps little children like the story of the little girl in the Bible who was dead. (St. Mathew 9:18-19, 23-25) He brought her back to life. What about the boy who had demon spirits in him and he would throw himself into the fire and the water and against the wall and hurt himself? (St. Mathew 17:14-18) Jesus healed him.

He cares for us. We need to care for Him and we need to care for ourselves. One sure way to prove that we love our parents is if we pray for them everyday of our lives. Please pray for your parents and your family because they always come and help you when you're in trouble. Don't forget that if it were not for your parents, you would not be here today.

I believe that my parents would give me almost anything I ask for if it's good for me; but nothing if it's not good for me. I don't ask them for very much because sometimes I see them doing so much for other people and I think that they may not have the money.

Another thing we should do as young people is pray for our parents' health so they can be strong and keep working and keep doing the things that they need to do. Then they can keep making money to take care of us and when they grow old we will take care of them.

So many kids are talking about running away from home because they have heard somebody say that the streets are good for them. We forget to read about all the children that are being killed in the streets. Some girls at eleven years old have turned into the "P" word on the street. That's really a terrible way to make money. I don't like to say the word but I think you know what I mean. Some young boys are taken and turned into "dope boys" or "runners."

I wish this wasn't true but it is and we must deal with it. As a Christian child I must pray for these situations that I see everyday before they become too bad for our society to handle.

I'm glad that my parents are who they are. My mother is a nurse. She works so hard and she is so pretty. I want to be just like her. My dad is a pastor, as you know, and boy does he work hard. He makes everybody else around him work hard, but he gets so much done. We all fuss about how much he fusses, but when we see the results we appreciate his position.

I want to be a hard worker in life like my dad, but I want to be mellow like mom. Dad's kind of aggressive. He's like "hyper" and sometimes it makes everybody else uncomfortable. We know he loves us and wants us to do well in life. So I can put up with my dad's attitude every now and then because he has to sign for my car when I turn sixteen. He has to take me to places because I'm not sixteen and I cannot drive for myself. He has to okay my boyfriends when I start dating. He's already asked me if I would stay with him and mom until I'm thirty years old. I didn't answer "yes" because my sister was asked the same thing and she said, "I don't think so." At about thirty years old she wants to have her own place. As for me I think I'll start a little earlier. Sorry Dad.

This is the kind of family that we have; lots of fun. You can have the same but you have to put Jesus in the middle of it like we've done. We all love Jesus. We all know that he's our number one and that we can do nothing without Him.

I think that every young person should sing in the church choir. I guess you would have to be in church to sing in the church choir. (HINT!!) I think that all of us have talents that we need to use. When we sing in the choir it's our way of showing God we love Him and that we want to praise Him and worship Him.

Now, some of our churches differ in the way we worship, but still we all believe that there is but one God. Why don't we take that and let that rule us instead of so many different denominations, so many different beliefs, and so many different people saying they're right and other people are wrong. I don't think that this is what God had in mind for us. I think He wants all of us to work together: all races, all creeds, and all colors. He wants all of us to help each other and to love each other. I may be a kid but I'm not kidding. I really love the Lord! I love Him because He wakes me up in the morning and He gives me strength in my body. He doesn't always let my daddy say "no." Sometimes, most of the time, my daddy says "yes" to things that I ask him for. I thank God for the Lord that's in my daddy's life.

*Genesis 8:21 ...for the imagination of man's heart is evil from his **youth**.*

*Proverbs 20:29 The glory of **young** men is their strength.*

OTHER KIDS' POINTS OF VIEW

I have a friend that has a different family than I do. Listen at what she has to say:

Hi, I'm Chrissy's friend. It appears that my family goes through a lot more changes than Chrissy does with her family. I used to live with my mom but now I have to live with my dad. I had to change schools, people who I knew, and friends. We also have a lot of arguments.

Sometimes my dad and stepmother will say things that they really don't mean (or I hope they don't mean). After they say them, later on they will say, "SORRY." I usually get hurt in all these things because I think I'm very, very sensitive and it hurts my feelings when they say mean things.

We have made it through the year and now we have another year to accomplish.

In listening to my friend, I have to let her know that everything is going to be okay as long as she stays with God. God always has a plan.

Now, I have another friend who is eight years old who wanted to share with me what hurts her. She told me that the thing that hurts is that her mom and dad don't live together because they're separated. She wishes that her mom and dad could get back together and all of them could be one big happy family.

I want to say to her that you never know what's going to happen. Your wishes may come true and if they don't it's always for a good reason.

I praise God that He's there for young people also. You can read your Bible everyday. Don't let the devil tell you that you can't understand the Bible. I guess it will depend on what you read. If you read the gospels and understand Jesus' doings then it'll help you. You can read the Psalms and Proverbs too. Sometimes the Old Testament scriptures are confusing when you're young and the devil will try to discourage you about the whole Bible, but don't be. Read the Bible like you do your clothes. If you don't feel like something is fit for the occasion, don't wear it that day but put it back in the closet. However, you know that you have something else that you can put on, so you keep looking until you find it.

I don't mean to sound like I'm a parent or anything. I'm just trying to get a message out to all of my readers that being a child, being a kid, or being young is not all bad. There are a lot of benefits. You get to give other people love and joy. Almost all of us have those uncles and aunts that love those cuddly hugs. Sometimes I don't really like them because they have mushy lips. You know what I mean.

I know they mean well, so I don't really say anything. I guess that too can be prayed about. What I'm trying to say is that everything can be prayed about. I don't think we're doing it though. We need to start praying more and more about the things that concern us and about the things that the devil wants us to do that's bad. For everything he wants us to do that's bad God has so many things He wants us to do that's good.

I would rather please God than please the devil. The Bible says, in Hebrews 11:6, that if we please God we can get rewards, but we've got to have faith. In Proverbs 16:7 it says He'll make our enemies settle down and leave us alone. That's why it's called the "good news" because that's good news. All of us should practice the art of "dropping a dime or quarter", (making a phone call) and giving somebody the "411" about the Bible for the day, sharing a scripture verse, or letting someone know everyday that God loves them and you love them.

Sometimes a hurting child just needs to know that he's loved. It doesn't always have to come from adults. We can help each other. We can tell each other that we love one another and we don't have to mean boyfriend and girlfriend love. It could be sisterly or brotherly love in the Lord. I'm getting the feeling that you might think that I'm trying to be a parent, not really. I just want to write something to help somebody else. I want to thank all of you for loving me. I love you too. You're my friends. We get along sometimes. Sometimes we fall out with each other, but it never holds for long because we all have - guess what? You guessed it, "attitudes."

Attitudes can do so much to hurt a good situation. Someone can have a birthday party and we can be having fun. One person can come in with an attitude and then he'll start talking to other people about other people who talk about people who talk about people and it goes on and on. Then everyone will be talking about each other and the party will be messed up because of - guess what? You've got it, an attitude.

I really want everybody to pray about attitudes so we can grow up to be like Jesus. I'm so glad He did not have attitudes because He may have chosen not to die on Calvary and then what would we do? We have enough sin in the world to deal with already than to deal with Jesus not being there for us.

Let me apologize for my first point of view being so long. The second view of salvation that I want to talk about is *repentance*. I told you I was going to talk about five points: confession, repentance, faith, regeneration, and also the scripture. Well, let's talk about repentance. My daddy preached one time that repentance is not penance. There I was confused again. Later he taught me that penance is when you try to do a deed for something that you've done or you try to trade something in. For instance, if somebody tears up your dollhouse they may bring you some jack stones to replace it. That is penance. Repentance is different.

Repentance must be done in your heart and in your soul and in your mind. You have to say to God, "Lord, Jesus come and save me. I am guilty of the Adam sin but save me. I also have some other things that I'm guilty of; lil' bitty things that may not matter to other people but they matter to you. So I bring them to you and tell you that I'm sorry for what I have done that is against your will." Now that's repentance.

If you have your Bible handy, turn to St. Mark 1:15. You will find these words, "...the kingdom of God is at hand: repent ye, and believe the gospel." I'm not going to try and make you believe that I understand everything there is about the kingdom of God because I don't. I think it means that the Lord is almost ready to come back and get His people. I do know that the phrase "is at hand" means it's close by. He tells us it is close to the time when God is coming back to get His people. So make sure that you pray everyday and tell God you're sorry for the sins that you have done so you won't be guilty like Adam and Eve were.

The Bible also says that we are to believe the gospel. Now that's a tough subject because everybody does not know what the gospel is. In my opinion the gospel is found in St. Matthew, St. Mark, St. Luke and St. John. I was taught that there are only four (4) gospels, but then my daddy preaches out of other books too: Acts, Romans, Hebrews, and all of the rest of them. I don't know if they're called the gospel or not but I do know that in St. Matthew, St. Mark, St. Luke and St. John (in my Bible) there are some red letters and those are the words that Jesus spoke.

Since Jesus is the key person in our lives, I think maybe we should really learn what He says about everything else because people do get things wrong sometimes. If we do not repent, I don't think we're going to make it to where Jesus is because he told us that we must do that in order to make it. (St. Matthew 3:2; St. Luke 13:3,5; 6:12) I'm going to pray for everybody and you pray for somebody too, that God will teach all of us how to repent, and just how to confess. I'm going to pray that God will help all of us to understand that it's not about playing like we're praying, getting on our knees and not being serious. It's about meaning business and really telling God to forgive us of our sins because of what we received from Adam and that we don't want to go to the devil's place, but where Jesus is.

My third view on salvation is *faith*. In Hebrews 11:1, (almost everyone knows this scripture), it says that faith is the substance of things hoped for and it's the evidence of things not seen.

Please do not be upset with me because I refer to my daddy's teaching so much, but that's all I really know. He's a good preacher and a good pastor and I believe that he teaches me well. He taught me that faith is having what you need in your heart, in your mind, and in your soul although you may not have it in your hand, in your closet, or in the bank. Then you will always be satisfied if you don't get what you ask for (I think I'm close enough).

The scripture that I want to share with you on faith is found in St John 3:14-36. There's a lot in there. I'm going to read it and read it and read it so I can understand it. In St. John 3:14-15 it says, "And as Moses lifted up the serpent in the wilderness, even so must the Son of man be lifted up: That whosoever believeth in him should not perish, but have eternal life."

When the children of Israel were in the wilderness and they were almost ready to die, God told Moses that if he would build this thing that looked like a serpent, put it on the tip end of a stick and hold it up in the air, then everyone that would obey Moses by looking at the serpent would get help and would be healed. Many of the people did exactly what they were asked to do. Then you had some that thought they would challenge what they were asked to do and so they didn't look. They died in the wilderness.

Well Jesus died on Calvary. When we are told to lift up Jesus it really means that we're supposed to talk about how we appreciate Him and how we admire Him for dying for us on Calvary. The Bible says that if we were to do this we could get the same results that they got in the wilderness when Moses lifted up the serpent and all who looked, lived.

You've got to do this by faith. This is not something you can just say you do. Too many young people do not understand salvation, confession, repentance, or faith.

All of us have had a day when we really had to believe God for something. Maybe you didn't study as you should have and you were facing an "F." You had to pray and ask God for help and then you had to believe that He would help. This is a type of faith right here.

The Bible has a lot of scriptures on the word faith. Hebrews 11:6 is a very important one. It tells me that if you don't have faith you can not make God happy. You've got to want to make God happy. If you don't have faith you can't make God happy because the Bible says that faith is God and God is faith. When I talk to you about the views of salvation my message is that we need to confess the sin of Adam which we inherited and repent of the sins that we do on our own. We've got to believe in our hearts, souls, and minds that God is going to do what He says He's going to do when we repent of our sins.

Now let's talk about this big word *regeneration*. You may know this as born again. Sometimes you ask people if they are born again and they don't know what you're talking about. Then you ask them if they are saved and they still don't know what you're talking about. But then when you ask them if they have the Lord in their lives they always say "yes." Just having the Lord in your life may not be enough. Every man has Him in their life in that they exist. This does not mean that He controls their lives.

I think that it is important to share the definition that I got out of the Webster Dictionary for the word regeneration with my readers. It means to bring back to life again. It means to cause a person to be born again spiritually. I guess we could just say that since Adam and Eve messed it up for us, Jesus came to clean it up for us. When this happens it is called regeneration.

Now my fifth view of salvation is on the word *scripture*. In 2 Timothy 3:15, it reads, " And that from a child thou hast known the holy scriptures, which are able to make thee wise unto salvation through faith which is in Christ Jesus."

God wants us to study the Bible just as much as our teachers want us to study our homework. They know that if we do not study, we won't learn and if we don't have knowledge of what we're dealing with in life we will be easily led astray.

The Bible says that Satan takes advantage of us when we are ignorant of his devices. (2 Corinthians 2:11) So studying has to be part of our everyday schedule. Believe me, I know it's not going to be something that you're going to automatically want to do. I struggle with trying to study myself. Reading gets so boring but I'm sure that's because the devil wants us to concentrate on things that are bad for us. He wants us to see the things that are good for us as boring. We've got to be careful of his little tricks and games.

When we look at everything that I've written so far in this chapter we'll see that God has made it very easy for us to be successful people. We must become spiritual. We must confess our sins daily, repent of them, and have faith to believe that God is going to help us with them. We should expect our regeneration to take place because He said it would and then we must stay in the scriptures, studying the word of God more than any other book.

Different churches view salvation in different ways. I guess we all need to understand that we need God. I think that the total point of the salvation message is that we're in trouble and that we need someone to rescue us. We have fallen into the water and drifted into the deep and we need a lifeguard. I think it's kind of neat to look over to the side and see Jesus sitting at the table with His legs crossed looking over the pool just in case someone gets into the deep water. If they do, He will dive into the water and save them. That's His job on earth to save people that are dying.

I guess we have a part in this too. Once we have been saved from our dying state we need to stop playing in the deep water. We should make sure we stay in the shallow water so that we won't get ourselves in trouble.

This is how I think it happened. God created the heavens and the earth and all of the things, like bugs, trees, fish, and birds. Then He created male and female. Then He took them and formed them out the dust but they weren't moving so He breathed into their nostrils the breath of life and they became living souls. Then he put them in the Garden of Eden and they were doing okay for a while. Eve drifted away and went for a walk and the serpent tricked her into eating what God told her not to eat. Some people say it was the devil but the Bible called it a serpent. Then she took what she was eating to Adam and he ate some too. God told them that they should not eat from the tree of knowledge of good and evil, but they disobeyed him. The serpent told Eve that God didn't really mean it when He said she would surely die. So she thought maybe she wouldn't die if she disobeyed

God. She ate of the fruit and gave it to Adam. God put them out the garden. They were in trouble then.

When my dad and I were talking about this story, we talked about a "cloud of sin" that was over their heads. God looked down and saw it and thought that He should send Jesus to take it away. So that's why He came, to take away that "cloud of sin." So He died on Calvary to pay the price for mankind's sin. If you don't receive him in your heart you still have to pay your own ticket for sin, which is death. The most important thing is you have to receive him into your heart if you want him to purchase your ticket for you. But Jesus will pay the ticket and then He'll give you life everlasting. (St. John 3:16)

When you get saved and start growing in God, all you have to do is just hang in there until God comes back. Keep repenting if you do wrong. When God comes back, the flesh part of us, the human part of us won't go to heaven but the soul will. That's the part that Jesus is in a relationship with. Let's keep our relationship with him in a saved state.

My favorite scripture is St. John 3:16. I used to wonder how God could save everybody but now I know. He is so big and regardless of how old or young, tall or short, big or skinny you are, He can save whomever He will. If you are black or white or whatever color, it doesn't matter to Him. He loves all men the same. When you get saved you don't ever have to worry about perishing because He'll give you eternal life. That's what Adam and Eve had at first before they disobeyed God and was put out of the Garden of Eden. We are saved and growing in God. We are learning how to live the life that will lead us right back to where Adam and Eve were at the beginning, a position where we'll never have to die anymore.

I'm scared of dying and I know that most of you are, I guess it's all right. It's supposed to lead to a "cool" place of living afterwards, heaven. Then I guess it's not so bad to die. We'll just have to wait on that time. It's not something I'm looking for so don't try to rush me. I'm just writing a book. I'm not trying to be a memorial.

A lot of older people say that they are ready to die but if you go to the hospital you'll see them crying in their beds and asking people to pray for them. I guess they didn't know that death could be that frightening. These are things I think that God will straighten out in us as we get older.

We've got so many other things to think about, like which color to wear with another color. Styles are constantly changing and our parents do not want to give up the money. We've got to worry about convincing them that every time we ask for something we ought to get it. If you come up with the formula, please share it with all kids everywhere in the world so we all can go to our parents and get everything that we want. I don't think this is going to happen so we better just settle for being saved and living for God.

If we confess to the Lord it's much easier than confessing to a human being because we can't trust everyone. Not everyone can keep a secret. Romans 14:11 is basically saying that God's "the man" and everyone should bow down to Him only and confess to Him only. From the Ten Commandments (Exodus 20:3-4), commandments 1 and 2 tell us not to have any other gods before Him or any graven images. If we study these commandments we'll understand this scripture. Some people worship famous people and that's not what we're supposed to do. Some people have graven images such as many cars or even sculptures.

Make sure you read this chapter over and over again everyday because I really want everybody to know about Adam and Eve, the serpent, God and Jesus, confession, repentance, forgiveness, and studying. I want everybody to know about how good God is and His love for people. So we've got to keep rehearsing it.

How are you enjoying this book so far? Now, let's get into the "world of attitudes."

ADJUSTING THE "TUDE" (ATTITUDE)

Attitude: A. A manner of acting and feeling that shows one's disposition.

B. A position assumed by the body in connection with an action of feelings.

Both parent and child need to learn the art of attitude adjustment. With no disrespect intended, I would like to say that it is just as easy for us to have bad days as teens and young adults as it is for our parents. This understanding is necessary if we intend to get along and if our goal is to give God the glory in our relationships.

I know that there is a lot of pressure on our parents. They have so many responsibilities and a lot of things they have to do. Sometimes when they're tired I think that they jump on us with their attitudes unnecessarily. Their patience is short and sometimes we do what they call "get on their nerves". I wonder if they ever think about the fact that we have nerves too?

I guess it would only be fair if we were to explain that sometimes we have nerves that are gotten on as well. Here are some of the times we are bothered by what our parents and other adults do. 1) Often we are told that we can't go places. When we ask the question why, we're told, "Don't ask me why; just do what I say. I'm your uncle. I'm your aunt. I'm your momma. I'm your daddy." I just don't think that this is fair. I think that there ought to be conversation and communication. 2) I think that we can do really well as friends if we were allowed to ask the questions (in respect), "Why are you telling me 'no' when I would like for you to say 'yes'"?

We don't always know how to respond to our parents' satisfaction. Sometimes what they see as an attitude is not what we mean to show as an attitude. I don't think it's fair to ask our parents to be perfect. The Bible gives us the responsibility of praying for our parents and our parents the responsibility of praying for us. It's all our jobs and I wouldn't trade my parents in for anything.

I can deal with the times I think they get on my nerves because I know that at times I do the same to them. Since we are on the subject of getting on each other's nerves, I guess we need to add in the facts of attitude. When one has had enough, gotten tired, and decided that he has reached his limit, he must be careful that he does not allow his attitude to control the rest of the day.

The Bible shows us through Jesus' example that adjustments in life are vital. All of us, especially those of us who are young and just starting off in life, must learn how to adjust our attitudes to the moment. For instance, if something happens in the morning and you are still pouting about it in the evening, you have not done a good job at adjusting your attitude.

If we don't adjust our attitudes it can leak over into our dealings with other people and cause an unnecessary problem with them. Other people do not deserve to be affected by our attitudes. That's why we need to communicate with our parents when there is a problem. We need to listen to what they have to say and hope and pray that they will listen to us. The best thing to do, I believe, is to hope and pray. We should pray this prayer:

Dear God,
Help me to catch and control my attitude before it makes me disrespect somebody else because then I may get busted by my parents. Amen.

It's not good when a child disrespects a parent. I wonder how many of us have thought about just how many times we have hurt our parents' feelings and offended them because of our attitudes toward something that they asked us to do or something that they disagreed with about what we wanted to do? They have feelings also and so we need to pray for them. I really mean pray. Don't think about praying but actually call your parents' names in prayer to God through Jesus and ask Him to keep them "cool" so they won't be worried and concerned about our attitudes.

There are a whole lot of special people in our lives. Some very important persons in our lives are teachers. They really have a tough job. There are so many children to deal with and so many attitudes to manage. For instance, when we get ***"unnecessary"*** bad grades. To tell the truth, all along we know when we are not doing our homework. We know that we are not paying attention in class. We know that we are not studying but there is something about the Corn Flakes that we eat ☺ and the popsicles that we lick ☺ that make us think that we can get by doing nothing, especially our homework. It doesn't work that way. If we are to be successful in life then we'll have to study more and pay attention in class.

Do you remember the day when your teacher handed you your paper? It was graded and at the top of the paper was an "F", a flag, flunk, fail. Do you remember that feeling? Do you remember that anger? Do you remember that disappointment? I do. Many of my readers probably remember when they had to deal with the fact of having to take that bad grade home and showing it to our parents. We really got nervous, so we got an attitude and guess with whom? You guessed right, the teacher. But was that fair? I don't think so! She didn't do anything to deserve our attitudes.

While I was on my way home to parents who were going to be upset and angry, and I was going to have to suffer punishment for a bad grade, I looked for somebody to blame the bad grade on and guess who I blamed the bad grade on? You guessed right again, the teacher. So I started getting my game together. I knew what I would tell my parents, "She doesn't like me. She picks on me. She has a bad attitude and mom you can ask the rest of the kids. Just the other day...."

As you may have figured out by now, my parents told me to "hush" or "shut up." The last statement is not popular in 1998 but it's still being used. It was very clear to me that my parents were not buying my game. They felt "chumped out" and lied to. After the third hour of sitting in my room with no phone, TV, music or visits from my friends, I started talking to myself. All along I had been talking about others that I was mad at. I ask myself the question that I always ask, "Why didn't you just do right? The homework was so easy."

Have you been in this situation before? It's at this time that we must be very careful because the devil will really work with us and try to make us feel sorry for ourselves and make us feel that somebody is picking on us. We must do the right thing.

The truth is we deserved that bad grade because we didn't do what we should have done. It wasn't the teacher's fault so we have to ask God to forgive us for being mad at her. It was not our parents' fault for being upset with us. They have that right because they teach us better than that. We will have to pray about the things we think and say behind their backs.

I know what we should do. Do you mind if I share it with you? We should do better and never make a bad grade again. This will make everybody happy. The teacher won't have to deal with us rolling our eyes. Our friends won't have to put up with our bad attitudes. We will not disrespect our parents and we will be much happier ourselves. If we don't do this, we will stay mad at our teacher. That's when the teacher will start paying for this terrible thing that she has done by giving us a bad grade when we failed to study or do the homework assignment that she gave us to do.

When we walk into the classroom the next day after a bad grade the first thing we do is look at the teacher and roll our eyes. Then we take our seat and every time she looks our way guess what we do? You guessed right. We roll our eyes again. And would you know that that would be the day when she calls on you to do something special in class. By now the attitude is so big that regardless of what she says or does, your response is going to be nasty and rebellious. Now there's a word that we really need to pray about, rebellion.

An attitude with the teacher can last all year. The fact that she does not deserve it doesn't change the reality that we give it to her. Sometimes we let the teacher off the hook in three, four, maybe five days but then she'll have to be careful. The least little thing that she does will add to the fact that she gave us an "F."

I pray and I trust that all of my readers will pray that God will help us not to think like this because it's wrong. We could all make "A's" because we are the Master's kids and Jesus is our big brother. He said in Philippians 4:13 that we can do all things through Christ which strengthens us but we've got to let Him in. He does not work very well with attitudes. We need to learn how to let the teacher off the hook. She's only doing her job. We'll have to learn how to let our parents off the hook. They're only doing their jobs.

What is it that teachers really want from us and for us? They want "A" students and for us to be bright and smart. Most of all, our teachers want us to be successful. I may not know how to really explain my position on success but I know that if I take what my teacher is trying to give me, later on in life when it's time for me to get a job (don't rush me daddy), I'll have what it takes to qualify.

Now, can a person who wishes this kind of thing for us be bad? The answer is "no!" Then what is it or who is it that makes us think that our teachers are so bad and are against us? The answer is the devil when he influences our attitudes. He also does this where our parents are concerned.

Sometimes our attitudes make us feel that we want to run away from home, do drugs, have sex and then have babies to get back at our parents. We have no idea what we're doing when we have attitudes so we had better watch ourselves during this time. My daddy says, "anger blurs discretion", I'm not sure what he really means by that. I think he means you can-not make good decisions when you are mad. Forgive me daddy if I've gotten you wrong, you know I love you!

Bad attitudes are made up by the devil. He doesn't just want you to be mad at your parents or teachers or friends. He won't stop until he puts you in jail or causes you to kill someone or worst of all, kill yourself.

Suicide is rated very highly among kids my age. This tells me that there may very easily be a communication problem between our parents and us. Why can't we talk to each other? The answer is our attitudes and our failure to adjust them.

Parents know more than we know. Although we don't always think that it is true. One thing that parents may not know is that things have changed.

Peer pressure is much different than what it used to be. There are more things to get into trouble with now. There are more places to go now than then. I guess what I'm trying to get everybody to do is to work together.

Jesus worked with all kinds of people. He worked with good people and bad people. He worked with spiritual people and unspiritual people. Certainly, we can work with each other.

We can get some serious attitudes with our older brothers and sisters but we want them to know that we do love them. They've got to back up just a little and let us try and live our lives without a whole lot of pressure. For instance, why do they always think that they can treat us like they are our parents? It's because they are "types" of parents but we haven't received them as that. You see, to us they're just our big brother or sister. They're not momma and daddy. Now I'll have to admit that when my sister tells me to do something, it's always for my good. I'm not quite clear yet why it doesn't always feel good but when I sit down and think about it, I always hear her saying, "I'm not going to let you make the same mistakes I've made in life." Some kind of way that sounds like she means well. I'll have to ask God, in prayer, to help me understand why it doesn't feel good when it is intended to be so good.

One of my main reasons for trying to write about attitudes is because they are contagious. One person's attitude goes to another and then that person has an attitude with someone else and someone else has an attitude with another person. For instance, my daddy fusses at me for making a bad grade. I get an attitude with him. When my mother comes home, the kiss and the hug that she normally gets she does not get today because I have an attitude. Then she asks me, "What's wrong?" I tell her, "Nothing!" Now she's getting an attitude because she knows that I'm lying to her but because she's had a hard day and her patience is not very long, she does not intend to play with me about my attitude. She gets an attitude and sends me to my room. All of a sudden, I hear this voice, "And you had better clean up your room!" Then I hear another voice, "Do not turn on the TV!" Then I hear another voice, "Have you washed your face and brushed your teeth today?" Then I hear another voice, "Do not talk on the telephone!" Then I really have an attitude. So when my sister knocks on my door I yell, "WHAT?" Then she gets an attitude because I'm yelling at her and she yells back, "Do not yell at me little girl!" And then daddy hears her yelling at me and he yells at her for yelling at me. And then mommy yells at daddy for yelling at her for yelling at me. And now everybody has an attitude. The dog starts barking and altogether we yell at the dog and say, "Shut up or get out!"

All of us, in our spirits, hear someone laughing. Who do you think could be laughing at a time like this? You guessed right, the devil, the master of attitudes. I want to challenge all who read this book to pray about our attitudes and make adjustments so that we can learn that it's proper to show emotion but it's not good to have negative attitudes.

Teachers mean well. Parents mean well. Brothers and sisters mean well and even though they maybe young, sometimes we don't take the things they say very seriously.

Ever since he, the devil, has been on earth, he has been trying to make people mad at each other. He tried to tempt Jesus but he wasn't very successful. He tries to tempt us and we need to pray that God will give us the strength so he won't be successful.

Adults say that we will grow out of our attitude phase. I will be glad when I do because I like Jesus too much to keep getting in trouble. Oh, did I forget to tell you that attitudes could affect the way you respond in church? If you don't fix them and make the proper adjustments then you will go to church with the same attitude that you have in school or at home. You know that Jesus does not deserve our little attitudes. *Dear Lord, please help us to adjust our attitudes and learn how to deal with life more maturely.*

It's not easy being a kid but I'm not kidding when I tell you that I love the Lord. I believe that anything that I bring to Him that is a concern of mine, He can fix it and He can take care of it for me. Sometimes I forget to pray. That's not good. We must always remember to pray. In St. Luke 18:1 it says, "...men ought always to pray, and not faint." I think faint means get tired because sometimes, as young people, we get tired of being told what to do and although it's good for us, it still can get on our nerves. So, you see it's not easy in this world but I believe that we can make it. I believe that we are God's children and if we just get closer to Him then He'll give us the strength we need to make it through.

Don't let your friends tell you that He's not worth it because He is. If anyone reading this book needs help, I would be glad if you would write me and ask me questions about being saved. I'll give you what I know. I'll share with you my knowledge. While it may not be very much, I believe that if Jesus gets it He can turn it into a whole lot.

I want to take this time to write about different kinds of hurts. I believe that we overlook the hurts that we do towards other people and we know that so many times people overlook the hurts that they do unto us. Sometimes what is simple to one person is not so simple to another.

I'm sure I have hurt my parents at times with my attitudes and with things that I do that I should not do, but there are times also when I have been hurt by my parents. For instance, my daddy and I had an experience that I want to share with you because this experience caused me some hurt. I've been healed from it now, but I think if I share my experience it may help you to go to your dad and share with him some things that he has done that may have hurt you. Although he didn't mean it, that did not change the fact that it hurt.

The situation happened when I was about ten years old. My cousin and I were playing outside and we found a frog. We named it Oscar. We played with Oscar for a little while but when it was time to go to bed we had to put him away. My dad told me to put him in a bucket. When I asked him if we should turn the bucket upside down so Oscar wouldn't get out he said no because the bucket didn't have any holes for him to breathe. Now that's true, but when we came back outside the next morning to get Oscar, he was gone. It would have been easy for me to blame my dad for Oscar getting away but Dad was actually right. If I had turned the bucket upside down then the frog would have died. I would much rather Oscar run away than be killed. Although no one was really to blame, I felt hurt. Maybe hurt is a part of life.

A KID-O-GRAM

Don't forget you're not supposed to judge a book by its cover.

We are growing up and we are getting there. It has taken a little time but I've already made it through thirteen years.

My goal is to catch up with you!

Mom, Dad, please leave money on the dresser, increase my allowance, and decrease my chores.

P.S. Words of wisdom, "It's no joke... kids are broke."

Reality In A Dream

At this point I would like to ask you to come dream with me:

I have been placed on a rather small stage. My seat is directly in front of a podium where my index cards that have my topics have been placed. I have some subjects I want to discuss. I think that maybe I can say something to help all of these young people during their critical times.

While standing in front of the podium going through the preliminaries, I look as far as I can see. My eyes land on the faces of sad, mad and depressed teens with all kinds of problems and serious issues that I hope to help.

> **I have been placed on a rather small stage.**

Directly behind all of these kids is the bright and shining sun. **So I think to myself, " I wonder if that's God's message to all of us that He's available and prepared to help us when we have problems?** There is not only the sun but also all of creation: the moon at night, the rain for dry seasons, and the wind in the autumn to blow the leaves away. All of these are God's signs that He is available to help us in our time of need."

> **So I think to myself, " I wonder if that's God's message to all of us that He's available and prepared to help us when we have problems?**

This group of young people has so many problems. You name it they have it. I mean really serious issues: drugs, pregnancies, runaways, alcoholism, and kids that are depressed and confused. They're standing there before me with hungry faces. Their eyes are fastened on me waiting for me to say something that can give them just one ounce of hope. How I pray that God will help me to help these young people.

Many of them are my same age. Some are younger and some are older. I can only thank God that I'm standing here and not out there. Why have I escaped so far? Why haven't I refused to yield so far? It's not because I'm good or special or different from all the rest of the kids. For some reason God has chosen to allow me to love Him and to have good parents that I can communicate with and who help me and lead me and guide me in the way I should go.

> **My parents' concern is that I seek them for security.**

My parents help me to deal with my being different. **My parents' concern is that I seek them for security.** I seek them for my needs when I'm without. I know they're going to give me the things that I need so I've decided that it's only fair that I allow them to leave me in the areas that I want to be: rebellion and bull-headedness. I may not agree with them but I must admit that they do have me in their best interest.

> **I've got a job to do. The older generation calls it "a charge to keep and a God to glorify."**

Well, it's time for me to start my speech. I'm a little nervous but when I look at the faces in front of me my nervousness doesn't matter. I just pray that I'll have a word from the Lord to share with these people. I start off by saying, "Hello, I'm Crystaline Joi Prothro." That doesn't seem to matter to them. They don't move and they don't clap. They're not impressed with who I am by way of my name. I guess this is a message for all of us that who we are, what our names are, where we live, and who our parents are, are not the important things in life. It's what our purpose is as it relates to other people. How we contribute to the needs of other people and how we can help other young people is what it's all about.

So I'm not going to get discouraged because they did not clap their hands. **I've got a job to do. The older generation calls it "a charge to keep and a God to glorify."** All of a sudden out of my mouth come the words, "It's going to be okay." I repeated it; "It's going to be okay as long as you stay with the Lord."

From the back, this young boy, maybe about 14 years old stands up. He has a hairstyle that is really, really weird and he has his nose pierced. He asks a question, "How can you tell us that it's going to be okay if we stay with the Lord when we don't even know who the Lord is?"

It is then that I come to realize that the first thing I must do is to invite the Lord into the lives of all these young people. Now I know that some of my readers may say that I should've talked first and then invited them but I hear that young boy's cry, "If somebody would just teach me I would receive him." Then I tell him the story that was shared with me when I got saved:

> **Many accept Him and many reject Him.**

Adam and Eve sinned against God and their punishment was death. Every man from every race and color would have died without hope of eternity, but God being the merciful loving God that He is, did not like this idea. So He sent Himself as Jesus in the form of man to earth, to teach men and women, and boys and girls to change their lifestyles and accept the fact that they are sinners because of Adam and Eve. They don't have to remain that way if they will accept Him, Jesus. **Many accept Him and many reject Him.**

> By faith I believe I'm changed. Amen.

Those who have accepted Him have Him in their lives now as their Lord. Those who have not accepted Him do not know Him as their Lord. He's still available. There's still time for the rest of us. I can see the young boy, as tears begin to roll down his eyes, and I ask him to raise his hands and repeat after me. Then I say to the rest, if anyone else wants to be saved repeat after me as well. I say, *"Lord, today I recognize that I am a sinner because of the Adam and Eve situation but I don't want to die and go to the devil's place. I want to live with you forever. So forgive me of my sins, my part in this matter, and come into my life and save my soul. I receive you as my Lord.* ***By faith I believe I'm changed. Amen.****"* Things get kind of aggressive. The crowd kind of has mixed responses. Some are clapping and others are moaning and shouting, "Go home! Go home!"

At this point I think that I had better continue my message. I remember that I left off telling everyone that it will be okay as long as they stay with the Lord.

I feel much better now because at least one soul has gotten saved. My energy level picks up, my smile becomes brighter, even my hope grows. My faith begins to spread out.

> **Her mother is on drugs, her daddy is in prison and her family doesn't really want her.**

I begin to get a little personal. Here are the words that I say, "I have some friends that are here today (some close friends) that are going through some very serious problems. I want you to know that I love you and that I'm here for you." A little girl about 10 years old jumps up and shouts very, very loudly, " Do you love me too? Will you be my big sister?"

I stop. Tears roll down my face. I look at her and wonder why this young kid is out here by herself? Then someone informs me, by handing me a note, that she is a runaway. **Her mother is on drugs, her daddy is in prison and her family doesn't really want her.** So I ask her to come up to the podium. When she gets there I just give her a hug and she hugs me. She is really dirty but that doesn't matter. I just want her to stay with me for the rest of my time there. I ask her if she will sit on stage with me. You should see her eyes and the smile on her face. Boy, I really start feeling special. There is a boy that wanted the Lord and received Him, and a little girl

> **Love is so vital to us.**

that only wanted to be loved. **Isn't that what all of us want, to be loved?**

When we run to drugs and alcohol aren't we saying that we just want to be loved? When we are rebellious, are we seeking negative attention so that we can get our parents to notice us? They're very busy you know: jobs, church, clubbing and dating, so they don't have a lot of time for us. Sometimes as young people we need to have them to not just say, "I love you," but show us that they love us.

Oh yeah, and let me say this, giving us money, clothes, etc. is not showing us that you love us but when you hug us and we feel your hugs, and even dads, when you hug your sons, it will not make them "sissies." Hug them. Please trust me, they want to be hugged. If you are a man and you teach them manly ways they're going to remain the same. **Love is so vital to us.** It's easy for a parent to yell, scream, and shout at us when we do wrong, but they seem to think

> **Isn't that what all of us want, to be loved? When we run to drugs and alcohol aren't we saying that we just want to be loved?**

that we can make it by ourselves without their hugs and kisses. We can't.

> **She thought that having sex was a fun thing to do and that it was just something everyone else was doing.**

I then addressed the crowd and asked a question. "How many of you, be honest, would love it if your parents would come right now and just sit down beside you and hug you?" You should see the hands that go up. Something automatic takes place. It seems as if when they raised their hands to say I want my parents to hug me that the tears begin to fall. This thing is beginning to feel really, really serious. I look over the crowd and there are some grown folks, but not a lot. I shout out, "I know that this is against the norm but everyone who's over the age of 18, I want you to mix into the crowd and I want you to hug those kids and let them know that they are loved." My daddy is really coaching me while he stands behind me on the stage. I really love him. He wants me to do well in life.

Finally, I look over the crowd and see a teenager. She looks to be maybe late 14 or early 15 years old, maybe even 13 but

> **We've got to come up with answers to our problems.**

she looks like she is about 7 months pregnant. She is crying her eyes out because she never thought she would be pregnant. **She thought that having sex was a fun thing to do and that it was just something everyone else was doing.** She never considered that inside of her she would be carrying another person. She has no job, no home and no family and she doesn't have the nerve (thank God) to have an abortion. Now she's pregnant and doesn't know who the father is; there were two guys involved. I tell her that I want to talk with her afterwards because some things are too personal to discuss in the open. You know what I mean? I don't want to talk about sex in front of all of those people.

My time is really running out so I think that I had better get down to business. Everyone is quiet and still listening and so I begin to talk. "There are many of you who have not had every problem that's here today and some of you have had almost all of them. Then there are others who really

> **"Start giving it up because your life is about to change."**

don't know whether they're going or coming. That's not the issue. **We've got to come up with answers to our problems."** Everybody claps. I really start feeling kind of special. My dad whispers in my ears, "Don't be prideful. Stay humble and just do the job God wants you to do." I look at him and shake my head as if to say "yes." So I continue. "I'm going to let you know that if you make goals for yourself and keep them you won't go through these problems. **We've got to have something to replace the bad things that we're doing.** (I feel boldness as never before.) Goals such as finishing high school, going to college, getting a decent job when you get out of college, getting married, and then getting pregnant. These are things that we must start thinking about." I ask them to close their eyes and think about some positive things that they want in life for 30 seconds.

I tell them that it doesn't matter if their choices are silly to them just as long as they make a choice to do something different. That's the beginning. Everybody stands in ovation at this statement. I think I hear my dad saying something but the crowd is too loud so I look at him. He says to me, "Say that again." So then I put emphasis on it and feel like Martin Luther King or some big speaker, and I say it again. Then I say, **"Start giving it up because your life is about to change."** (I must admit I do sneak a "hallelujah" in.) I go on to tell them that if they make bad choices that God will forgive them as long as they intend to do right, but they'll have to give their lives to Christ so that He can be in

> We've got to have something to replace the bad things that we're doing.

control.

Just ask Him for forgiveness and watch what He'll do. No matter how big your problems are, God will forgive you right now.

> **Reading the Bible is a very easy thing to do.**

Now even though I haven't gone through these things like many of you have. I'm still concerned about you and want to help you. I may be only 13 years old but I still know that I won't go through these problems if I stay with the Lord because He gives me other things to do, like reading my Bible. I hear an "aaah" like it is a boring thing to do. I think I had better address the issue a little. **"Reading the Bible is a very easy thing to do.** There are great stories in the Bible. History is in the Bible. The Bible teaches you how to handle situations. Every one of you has had situations that you needed to understand. For instance, the young lady that is pregnant over there without a husband, the same thing happened to Mary, the mother of Jesus. The people in the crowd said all kinds of bad things about her.

> **Just ask Him for forgiveness and watch what He'll do.**

I'm not trying to say that you are equal to her, but your situation is that you are carrying a child and you

> **I am only being kept by the mercy of God.**

do not have a husband. She was carrying a child and it must have been unbearable because no one really believed that she was carrying a child of the Holy Ghost. She had a tough time as well, but look at what she produced. She produced our Jesus and I'm sure that when you are finished with your pregnancy you will produce a beautiful child also. He or she will be a joy, not only to you but also to a lot of other people."

I get another standing ovation but I really do not want it because I really feel like it is getting out of hand and that they may start looking at me as if I am some type of god when in actuality I am just as they are. **I am only being kept by the mercy of God.**

I continue my speech by saying, "Now although we have goals for ourselves God also has goals for us. Some of these goals are: going to church as much as we possibly can, reading our Bibles, praying and witnessing to other people, and sharing with them our relationship with God. They can then come to God and get saved and God can help them with their problems. Then they will witness to someone else and the train will go on and on and on. If we do our part, other people will do theirs. Some will get saved and receive God in their lives. You can just tell how happy that is gonna make the world feel. When God sets our goals for us and we do the thing that He tells us, He

> **We may be young but we can get started now.**

will always be there to give us another chance if we mess up. God wants us to have goals for ourselves for two reasons (this is my opinion): 1) He wants us to be something in life to represent Him. My daddy preached a message that all of us are significant in some way or another regardless of what we think about ourselves. God made us important; 2) He wants us to make it to Heaven to live with Him. Now people are always disagreeing with where Heaven is. That doesn't really matter as long as I'm with Jesus I think that will be Heaven enough. **We may be young but we can get started now.** All we have to do is follow our own goals."

> **We should be careful whom we choose as our mentor.**

I warn the young people by saying, **"We should be careful whom we choose as our mentor.** Unfortunately all of us want to have athletes as our mentors or people that are rich and successful. I think this is a terrible thing that our world has adopted. Mentors, in my opinion, are supposed to be people who are deeply involved with God and have a relationship that will prove that God is their Savior. That is the #1 thing to do. Now if an athlete

> **My attention span is not that long and I get bored.**

falls in this category then by all means look up to them, but always consider what our athletes really believe in. Some of them worship idol gods and some of them believe in witchcraft and satanic practices. Not all of them do, some are really devoted Christians."

I remember how I am when I hear other people talk. **My attention span is not that long and I get bored.** I notice the crowd beginning to move a little and walking back and forth. I say to them, "Okay. I have said all I have to say. Now let us pray." I ask everyone to bow their heads. I look over at my dad and he gives me a "you did a good job" sign so I pray:

> **We may not always do right, but get inside of us, God, and protect us as your kids.**

"God we are here. Children, young people, and kids and we do not know what we are doing. We thank

> **We thank you for our parents.**

you that we exist, but I must say again we do not know what we are doing. We have not always been led right. Some examples that we are given to follow are not always proper and so we are left alone in many cases. We are misunderstood. We are neglected and overlooked. **We thank you for our parents.** *We are responsible for them as they are for us and we know that they will come to understand us, God, like you understand all of us. We ask that you will give us goals in our lives. Help us to be somebody in life, not necessarily to make a lot of money but to please you. Teach us to talk about our problems and God, right now, come into the hearts of all those that are not saved. Make a difference in our lives. I pray in your name, and we all want to let you know that we love you regardless of what and in spite of it all.* **We may not always do right, but get inside of us, God, and protect us as your kids.** *We really love you. Thank you Jesus. Amen."*

> **To my sister Precious I want to say, "Keep setting the example for me."**

What a crowd! I sit down and everyone is shaking my hand and hugging each other. We have had a wonderful time. It seems like we have been in church. I think I had better start doing things to help people. I know what I will do. I will write a book and I'll call that book *"I'm A Kid But I'm Not Kiddin' (Tru' dat) I Love The Lord"*. I will discuss things like kids have nerves too and youth is not a yoke so there is freedom. I'll address the question, **"Have y'all ever been young and if so then you know exactly what we are going through?"** Then I will promise my mom and dad that as I grow old I will put away childish things. I really believe that we can make an impact on the youth. I hope they, each of them, will read this book over and over again and give it to someone else. It may not cover all the questions of teens but it covers some. It may not be as mature as some want it to be or as childlike as others want it to be but it is what I feel in my spirit that I want to write and share, which is a contribution of significance to our youth and society. I love the Lord with all my heart, my soul, my mind and I am facing the biggest monster of all, life. I am not facing it by myself. I have God first, a loving father and mother, and a sister that I absolutely adore.

> "Have y'all ever been young and if so then you know exactly what we are going through?"

To my sister Precious I want to say, "Keep setting the example for me." I love it when you say to me, "Chrissy, I'm not going to let you make the same mistakes I have made." You have not shared them all with me but I will take your word for it, like I do when you say not to touch your stuff in your room or if I use your phone and don't put it back. I know that you will keep your word. I love you. Bye- bye.

*Ecclesiastes 11:9 Rejoice, O young man, in thy **youth**..*

*Joel 2:28 ...your **young** men shall see visions.*

*Titus 2:4 ...teach the **young** women to be sober...*

Setting goals is the first step to progress

Hello, I'm Shalisha Jackson, a 15-year-old teenager. I am so proud to be given an opportunity to write a piece in this book that should be a bestseller. There are some reasons, in case you want to know, why I think this book is the "bomb". First of all, Chrissy is a black 13-year-old young lady with her head on straight. Secondly, the information in this book is truthful and real. It is what's happening in our world. Adults write most books for youth but not this one. Our very own peer has tackled this task and completed it with truth and careful preparation. It is a great book, very encouraging and heartfelt.

> **Progress is the first step to achievement.**

I wish to share with you a point of view as it relates to setting goals and making progress. Again, I want to thank Chrissy for this opportunity to show my skills. I think I'm going to write a book also. I too have something to say.

To make progress is something very important in life. **Progress is the first step to achievement.** Achievement means I can strive for something and get it. Three goals that we must strive for and accomplish are:

> Having low self-esteem throughout a certain time in childhood can leave a scar.

1) The gaining of confidence.
2) Maturity in emotional situations.
3) Responsibility to take control of our weaknesses while working harder toward our goals.

To begin with, throughout our lives, many lessons are there to be learned. One that stands out is that it is impossible to truly believe in anything if you can't believe in yourself. Self-confidence has to be earned. This realization comes over the years, after long periods of self-doubt and unbelief. **Having low self-esteem throughout a certain time in childhood can leave a scar.** It takes time to realize that what is needed for guidance comes from within, and not from anyone else. As soon as we learn this lesson and apply it, our weaknesses, our issues, as well as conflicts that caused self-doubt, will start to disappear. This is known as a turning

> My mother told me that time brings us to maturity and gives us a different way of looking at situations.

point in life. You can see this as having already achieved something in life that maybe you were told that you could not do. This is a great achievement.

Another achievement to go for is to learn how to choose which problem areas to deal with and which to leave alone. Our past may be messed up with unnecessary arguments that could have been avoided with just a little amount of thought. **My mother told me that time brings us to maturity and gives us a different way of looking at situations.** Spiritual thoughts and simply putting yourself in the other person's shoes, turn out to be effective ways of getting your own point across, while receiving what the other person is trying to say to you. This is a great alternative to the screaming and yelling that has been the way of the past. This procedure can stop the heavy fights with parents (if applicable).

This is another sign of maturity, and the noticeable alleviation of former problems caused by simple one-sidedness. This is why I say that maturity and social education are marked as great achievements. One more achievement worth sharing is the responsibility that comes with working towards a goal. The time has passed for indecision, and has been replaced by the ability to

> **The decision about which goals to pursue is only the beginning.**

> **My achievements took time and education to accomplish.**

weigh a situation, and if it is a good one then we should jump on that "bad boy." To be successful, repeat the formula of getting rid of the bad one's and keeping the good ones. **The decision about which goals to pursue is only the beginning.** Having the strength and perseverance to follow through to the end is truly what I mean by taking responsibility.

The good and the bad that happens to you are what you accept and deal with or decide to do something about. Realizing that you have a part in your life's decisions is a step forward in growing up, which can be defined as another achievement. Accepting and learning to take action is another great achievement.

Basically, the achievements and realizations that have made life a learning experience are the stepping stones of progress. Achievements such as the gaining of confidence, maturity in emotional situations, and responsibility are the foundation to our

> **We should all be very proud of her because she represents a generation that is in a serious conquest with trouble.**

future success. Growing is reaching goals. **My achievements took time and education to accomplish.** This makes them all the more important and most importantly, they push me to greater accomplishments.

I'm older than Chrissy, the author of this book. I am almost 16-years old. I regard what she is doing as phenomenal and almost unheard of. **We should all be very proud of her because she represents a generation that is in a serious conquest with trouble.** This is a very good book and I pray for continuous success. Chrissy, keep up the good work.

                      Your friend,

                      Miss Shalisha Jackson
                      (15 years old)

Credits

I'm A Kid But I'm Not Kiddin' (Tru Dat)
was typeset by Robot Publishing and Hayah Documents.

Compositor	-	Robot Publishing Team
Manuscript Editor	-	Charmaine Johnson
Production Editor	-	Rosalynn A. Curry
Graphic Designer	-	Michael M. Smith

Copyright ©1998 by Robot Publishing

All scripture quotation unless otherwise indicated, are taken from the Holy Bible KJV.

All rights reserved. No part of this publication may be reproduced, stored in a retrieval system, or transmitted in any form or by any means-electronic, mechanical, photocopy, recording or any other except for brief quotations in printed reviews, without the prior permission of the publisher.